Dr Brighton's Indian Patients
December 1914 - January 1916

by Joyce Collins

CONTENTS

Cover: Royal Pavilion Music Room Ward 5
Opposite: 'Bal the little Gurkha, aged 17
whom the King and Queen paid great attention to at the Dome'

Brighton Books Publishing

Dr Brighton: 1750-1914

From the autumn of 1914, and throughout the war years, the Brighton local newspapers made frequent references in their headlines to 'Dr Brighton' and his patients - the wounded soldiers from the trenches in France who were brought for treatment in the many temporary hospitals established in the town. Between December 1914 and early 1916 some thousands of Indian soldiers passed through their own special hospitals and so became Dr Brighton's Indian patients. 'Dr Brighton' had been given his title long before, when the town developed a reputation as a health resort, elegant enough to attract wealthy patrons from among the aristocracy and gentry. The royal connection was strengthened when the young Prince of Wales - later Prince Regent and then King George IV - bought a modest farmhouse near the centre of the town and in time transformed it into the Royal Pavilion. The Pavilion was not popular with Queen Victoria and it was eventually acquired by the Brighton Commissioners.

Brighton continued throughout the nineteenth century to expand and, especially after the railway to London was opened, its population grew rapidly. Although the character of the town began to change, wealthy people continued to spend part or all of 'the Season' at Brighton, and the local papers on the eve of war in 1914 still published regular lists of visitors staying at the hotels and boarding houses - a practice begun more than a century before. At its centre, and along the seafront, the town retained its fashionable air, and there were plenty of good shops, theatres and even a cinema, one of the earliest in the country.

There was plenty of work for tradesmen and artisans of all kinds, and above all for servants, in private homes as well as hotels. At the lowest end of the social scale, however, life could be very hard, especially if a breadwinner was injured, became ill or died. In spite of much philanthropic work, and the existence of various charitable organizations, a family could easily find itself reduced to poverty and, at the worst, removed to the Workhouse. The huge Poor Law Institution was at the top of a hill overlooking the town, and there the destitute were relieved, sick children might be treated and aged paupers lived out their days.

Throughout the town there were schools, including many private fee-paying establishments for the middle and upper classes. For the majority, however, the elementary schools provided basic instruction for children aged between five and fourteen. By 1914 brighter children might be awarded a scholarship and be able to take up a free place at a grammar school.

In the early months of the Great War, when Indian soldiers wounded at the Front were sent for treatment in Brighton, they would have found themselves in one of the three Military Hospitals established in the town. One was at the Pavilion, another in the old Workhouse (renamed the Kitchener Hospital) and the third was in the York Place schools. The experience of these men, first in the trenches and then as patients of Dr Brighton is told in the pages that follow.

Opposite: Indian wounded in the Royal Pavilion

Black Watch & Indians hold advanced sector of line near Facquissart Post guarding Calais

1914 The War in Europe & the Indian Army

On August 4th 1914 Britain declared war on Germany. The German army had crossed the Belgian frontier as a preliminary to attacking France, and Britain had a treaty obligation to defend Belgium's neutrality. France called on Britain as her ally for aid in resisting the German advance as the German armies overran Belgium and made the first incursions on to French soil.

The continental countries had long before introduced conscription and had large classes of reservists to call up. Britain, with no conscription, had fewer reservists and, though these and some territorial units were immediately mobilized, the British Expeditionary Force was small in numbers by comparison. At its core, however, was a tough professional army of well-trained soldiers. In addition, Britain's great strength was in her navy. Throughout the war it was responsible for the protection of convoys transporting men and munitions to the battlefields and for the defence of the Channel ports.

On the outbreak of war, the Dominions - Canada, Australia and New Zealand - at once expressed their support for Britain and their forces were later to play a vital role in France, at Gallipoli and in Mesopotamia. In 1914, however, the urgent need was for reinforcements to assist the French and British armies already in the field and it would take time for the Dominion forces to arrive. In Britain thousands of young men queued up to volunteer, but it would be many months before they could be trained and equipped. Only India - not a Dominion, but the 'jewel in the crown' of the Empire - had regular forces, ready and available to call on.

The Army in India always included some units of the British Army on temporary service. These were in addition to the Indian Army itself which numbered in 1914 some 155,000 men. Its main function was the defence of India, primarily on the North-West Frontier, but it could also, if need arose, be called upon for internal security or to provide up to two divisions for overseas expeditions. The decision was made on August 8th for the mobilization of two infantry divisions and one cavalry brigade for overseas service. The original intention was to use these forces to relieve troops on garrison duty in Egypt but in view of the situation on the Western Front there was a change of plan and the Indian Army Corps was re-routed from Egypt to Marseilles and began arriving there on September 26th, although it was not equipped or trained to fight against the might of the German army.

Decisions about the deployment of the Indian Army were made - of course without reference to the Indians themselves - by the Government of India. Quite different from the Indian Army were the Imperial Service Troops which were maintained by 27 of the Indian princely states. Quite independent of the Government of India, these were recruited from and commanded entirely by Indians. A telegram received in London on September 7th from the Viceroy, Lord Hardinge, gave details of the many offers of help from the princes. Two days later a statement by the Secretary of State for India must have sounded strangely exotic in the sombre chamber of the House of Lords. Among many others, Sir Partab Singh of Jodhpur, a distinguished Rajput, offered his state lancers. He was, in fact, himself to command them in the field. The Maharajah of Rewa asked 'What order has my King for me?' and volunteered the use of his troops and the gift of private jewels. There were other offers - of horses and money and a hospital ship, the 'Loyalty', for the expeditionary force. M K Gandhi - years later to become known as the Mahatma - himself offered his services and raised a Field Ambulance Corps.

The Secretary of State acknowledged with gratitude 'this demonstration of true and heartfelt loyalty in India to the King Emperor', and informed the House of Lords that the Viceroy had accepted from 12 of the States contingents of infantry, cavalry, sappers and transport, and also the Bikaner Camel Corps, and added that some of these had already embarked on active service. Even territories which were not under British rule also made offers of help. The Government of Nepal, an independent state under British protection, pledged resources and cash to provide the Gurkha regiments with machine guns and gave a donation to the India Relief Fund. In Tibet the Dalai Lama offered material help and the prayers of the Lamas.

These offers of help were obviously valuable and, in time, played an important part in the allied war effort, but already by September the immediate need was to reinforce the British sector on the Front. It was the Indian Army Corps which, within days of its arrival in France, was to provide that relief. The German war plan depended on a lightning offensive in France, and its army - a mighty instrument of war - was everywhere victorious and so near to Paris that the French Government had already left for Bordeaux. This was the situation when the Indian Expeditionary Force, the first ever to be sent to fight in Europe, was landing in Marseilles.

British wounded soldiers at the Grammar School

War Comes to Brighton

The last days of peace were being enjoyed by Brightonians and visitors alike. Four columns of the 'Brighton Gazette' for Wednesday July 29th were taken up with names of 'Latest Arrivals', and many titled people, clergymen and less eminent citizens filled the hotels and boarding houses listed. Some visitors probably took advantage of the express services being offered to 'delightful Dieppe' by 'most luxurious turbine steamers' (First Class: 21s 1d, Second Class: 16s 1d. or Third Class: 12s 1d). Lucky ticket holders taking a trip on Volk's Electric Railway could have a free flight in a seaplane from its station off the beach opposite Paston Place.

The day after war was declared the Newhaven-Dieppe cross-Channel boat ran for the last time. It was crowded with people of various nationalities trying to get back to their own countries while, on the return trip, the boat would bring British passengers waiting in Dieppe to get home. Not all those in Brighton of German origin took the opportunity to leave and the 'Gazette' noted that for some years the German colony in the town had been expanding, especially among hairdressers and hotel workers. A man with the un-English name of Jankewitz was warned of the extreme danger of loitering near any Government depot at the present time. One German (an alleged spy) was arrested.

The main concern in August 1914 was, however, the number of places available for the casualties that must inevitably begin arriving from the Front. Brighton, like other towns along the Channel coast, expected to receive many of the wounded. In 1914 there were only some 7,000 beds available in military hospitals in the whole country. By 1918 the number would be 364,133. There were many offers of accommodation in Brighton for additional hospitals, one of the most important being the grammar school in Dyke Road, whose pupils returned for the duration of the war to their former premises in Buckingham Road. The school was quickly transformed into the 2nd Eastern General Hospital and was equipped to take over 500 patients, with 18 doctors attached from local hospitals. The hospital was soon to receive its first patients, men of the 2nd Royal Sussex Regiment, wounded during the retreat from Mons.

4

300 wounded men arrived in Brighton on September 1st and these were shortly to be followed by the first parties of Belgian (and later French) refugees. The 2nd Eastern General Hospital was fully occupied throughout the war, receiving British soldiers and, later also, men from the Dominions.

All kinds of war work were being carried out in the town. At the Pavilion some of the Queen's Nurses (members of the Queen Alexandra's Military Nursing Service) were giving demonstrations of nursing while the Mayoress organized working parties in the King's Apartments, cutting out and sewing up garments. The St John Ambulance Association also had working parties for the collection and forwarding of clothing and gifts to the sick and wounded. Meanwhile, the casualty lists in each issue of the 'Gazette' grew longer. The confusion on the battlefield in the early days of the war was illustrated by the fact that many more names appeared as 'Missing' rather than 'Killed' or 'Wounded'.

Long before it was known that the Indian wounded were to be brought to Brighton (it was at first assumed that they would be sent to special hospitals in France), great interest was shown in news of the imminent arrival of the Indians in France. On September 12th the 'Gazette' reminded its readers that 'it must be remembered that it (the Indian Army) is not organized primarily for service out of India, and that the organization of so large a force for despatch overseas is a very considerable undertaking', adding that this was especially so with troops for whom special provision had to be made.

More schools and large private houses were now being converted into temporary hospitals. The elementary school in Stanford Road became a hospital annexe, and a Red Cross hospital with 33 beds and an operating theatre was established at 6 Third Avenue, Hove. The Battle of the Aisne, towards the end of September, produced more heavy casualties and the 100 beds put at the disposal of the War Office by the Royal Sussex County Hospital were soon filled. Some British and Belgian casualties were sent to the French Convalescent Home or occupied one of the three new wards opened at the Dyke Road Hospital. One Belgian soldier who died was buried in the Heroes' Corner at the Borough Cemetery. St Mark's Schools in Arundel Road were then requisitioned by the War Office, together with Howard House and two houses in Sussex Square for the use of the Red Cross and the Royal Army Medical Corps. There was, thus, a complex of buildings in Kemp Town, together known as the Kemp Town Hospital. At the other end of the town, 38 Adelaide Crescent, Hove, the home of Mrs Barney Barnato, widow of the South African millionaire, was converted into the Hove Military Hospital and could take 20 wounded soldiers.

The actual arrival in France of the Indians - 'large reserves of perfectly fresh and thoroughly trained troops' - was reported on October 28th. Three days later the 'Gazette' printed the first appeal for 'Comforts' for the Indian soldiers. With thoughts of the coming winter, a request was made for gifts of money, tobacco, pipes, cigarettes, tinder-lighters, belts, cardigans, mittens, gloves, mufflers, Balaclava helmets with ear-holes, handkerchiefs and socks. All these articles were urgently needed and the Mayor of Hove requested that they be sent to the Town Hall.

War work clearly occupied much of the time of many people, but it is interesting to note that in social circles the Season was in full swing. After church on the first Sunday in November, the Hove sea-wall presented an animated appearance . . . 'the gathering was essentially a smart one, and shewed that though war is with us in all its grimness it has not deterred aristocratic visitors from paying their yearly visit to the town, or spending the winter there in the usual way'. According to the agents, houses were letting fast. At the Royal Pavilion improvements had now been completed for the restoration of the kitchen and fitting new cooking appliances. Few of those carrying out the work could have known that these would soon be used in the service of the Indian wounded who were unlikely to enjoy 'the most elaborate dinner menu' recommended for big or small gatherings.

The main entrance to the Kitchener Hospital, taken shortly after the Indians had left

The Indian Military Hospitals in Brighton

In November came the news that the Indians wounded on the Western Front were to be sent to Brighton and that the Pavilion was to be taken over and converted into a military hospital. A high official of the War Office met the Mayor, the Chairman of the Pavilion Committee and the Town Clerk and suggested that if the inhabitants would give up to his Majesty the King the use of the Royal Pavilion, Dome and Corn Exchange for this purpose, it would be greatly appreciated. The Corporation readily agreed and the work of converting the buildings was completed in an astonishingly short time. The first contingent of wounded Indian soldiers arrived at the Pavilion just thirteen days after the request was received from the War Office.

The urgent need for hospital accommodation for the Indians arose from the fact that there had been a fire on one of the ships moored in Southampton Water to serve as temporary hospitals. As a result, the Indian sick were crowded into an adapted hospital in Southampton. On the following day the King came to inspect the hospital and saw the need for proper accommodation to be made available. He made Sir Walter Lawrence his Commissioner in charge of the Welfare of Indian Troops, with reponsibility to take action in the matter.

On Saturday November 21st Sir Walter, accompanied by Major PS Lelean (the high official from the War Office), paid a visit to Brighton and by 6 pm returned to London, having telegraphed to His Majesty that the Pavilion and Dome had been secured as an Indian hospital. Lelean was left to organize the transformation and the way in which this was carried out was described by him at the time. Noting that the Pavilion was a crowded museum, and the Dome had 1500 seats clamped to its tiers, he went on to say that during that same Saturday night he enlisted the help of Boy Scouts who cleared the seats and exhibits out. (The 'Gazette,' probably more accurately, referred to 40 'sturdy energetic young fellows', members of the Boys' Brigade.)

Straight away the next morning, a Sunday, Lelean employed local firms to fetch from London enough khaki-coloured linoleum to cover the entire floor area and this was laid the

6

same night. On Sunday, too, Lelean got a detachment of troops from the Sussex Yeomanry to handle the arriving beds. On Monday a quartermaster from the RAMC came to assist with the preparations. By Wednesday Lelean was able to send a set of photographs to the War Office, 'showing the Dome as a completed Hospital with radial beds around a centre embedded in tropical foliage'. The photographs were delivered to Lord Kitchener, then Secretary of State for War, who took them straight to the King. Both considered the arrangements made as excellent .

The 'Gazette' gave further details to its readers. The space around the Pavilion and the Dome was almost blocked with large boxes, marked with the Red Cross, full of blankets, packages of wadding, lint and medical supplies. More work was going on inside the Pavilion where a 'khaki-hued compo board dado' was being attached to the lower part of the walls of the Banqueting Room and the Music Room. The Dome and the Pavilion had already been fitted with an admirable system of artificial heating, but in the Corn Exchange, which was not so well supplied, it was thought the defect could be made good. Like the Dome, the Banqueting Room, the Music Room, the South Drawing Room and the Saloon were to serve as wards. Rooms upstairs were prepared for the Indian officers. Operating theatres were set up in the Pavilion kitchen and in the vestibule at the entrance to the Dome in Church Street. Close to the main entrance were an X-ray department and rooms for heat and electrical treatment.

There were to be other special provisions needed to meet the dietary and ritual requirements for men of different religions. Separate arrangements had to be made for Hindus, Sikhs and Muslims. There were to be nine kitchens serving the Pavilion/Dome complex, most of them in huts erected on the lawns. These would cater specifically for Muslims or for either meat-eating or vegetarian Hindus. Special arrangements were made for the ritual killing of animals and the storing of meat. There were separate places for washing up, for bath-houses and latrines. Preparations were also made for separate mortuaries. Since wards were to be mixed, there would be two water taps in each, one for Hindus and the other for Muslims. Before the first patients arrived, the Indian orderlies moved in and notices were prepared in Urdu, Hindi and Gurmukhi. One further essential requirement was provision for religious worship. A Sikh temple (known as a gurdwara) was erected on the Pavilion lawns and space was set aside on a grass plot in front of the Dome where the Muslims, then generally called Mohammedans, could pray facing Mecca.

All this was a useful beginning, but the lists of Indian casualties at the Front (the earliest units to arrive found themselves fighting in the first Battle of Ypres) were lengthening and, by November 1914, already numbered some 1800. Many who had been wounded earlier had been taken to Southampton and the nearby Netley hospital from which they were later transferred to Brighton. Some Indian soldiers remained in Hampshire. In the New Forest the Lady Hardinge Hospital, paid for and under the control of the Indian Soldiers' Fund, and the Forest Park Hotel, both at Brockenhurst, were designated for the treatment of the Indian wounded. Some Indians were cared for at the Mount Dore Hotel in Bournemouth. The Hotel Victoria at Milford-on-Sea and the camp at Barton both served as convalescent hospitals for Indian troops. In Brighton the 724 beds provided at the Pavilion, Dome and Corn Exchange, would make a useful contribution, but there was need for greatly increased accommodation.

All over the country workhouses, asylums, schools and other public buildings were being considered as possible military hospitals. It is not surprising, therefore, that Sir Walter Lawrence, having secured the Pavilion, turned his attention to the Brighton Workhouse at the top of Elm Grove and sought the cooperation of the Guardians to take it over. A telegram was sent to Lord Kitchener: 'The Guardians of Brighton Parish, being of the opinion that the Poor Law Institution and Infirmaries are admirably suited for hospital treatment of Indian troops, beg to place such institution at the disposal of his Majesty for that purpose'. The offer was accepted.

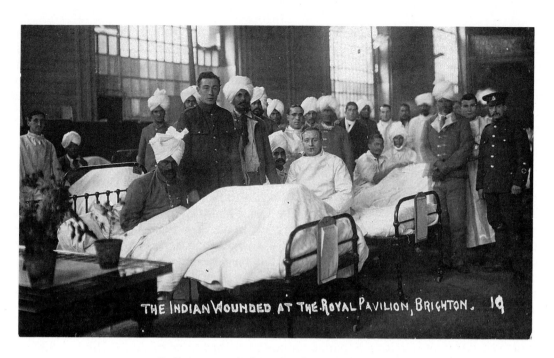

Indian wounded in the Corn Exchange

There was, however, the problem of what should be done with the present inmates. The sick children could be fairly easily transferred to the Royal Alexandra Hospital, but many of the old people were feeble and infirm and some were very sick. A special committee was set up to find solutions, and some of the aged inmates were returned to relatives or friends who could care for them. For the rest, plans were made to acquire properties that would provide temporary homes in the town or nearby villages. The 'Gazette' and the 'Herald' published at this time gave details of some of these arrangements. Reporters remarked especially on the good fortune of 97 old ladies from the Workhouse who found themselves occupying The Lawns, a luxury block of four houses along the seafront that boasted beautiful wood fittings, curious fireplaces and fanciful architecture - and even electricity and warm water. 170 of the old men were sent to Sussex House, at the top of Norfolk Terrace, and some of the very elderly were taken to Wivelsfield Hall. The inmates from the South Ward of the Workhouse were put into the Downs Hotel at Hassocks - 'much to the scandal of the local Parish Council, who have passed a resolution of horror at this profanation of their stately neighbourhood'.

Difficulties were also encountered in Kemp Town, where the neighbours of numbers 4 and 6 in Sussex Square objected to the arrival of 55 sick females and 55 sick males, respectively, and the people living in Eastern Terrace did not welcome the idea of 76 sick inmates being moved into number 5. 'The Guardians', said the 'Herald', 'have assured them that no infectious cases will be brought, and that no one in the neighbourhood will be able to notice the presence of the patients'. It seems that the owners remained obdurate and were threatened with the peremptory intervention of the War Office, if the appeal to their patriotism failed, since their objections were seriously delaying the steps necessary to prepare the Workhouse for the reception of the Indian wounded .

The huge task of vacating the Poor Law Institution and finding accommodation for nearly 1,000 sick and infirm people, including the very old and the very young, was in fact completed in three weeks. Nevertheless, this caused some delay in completing the transformation from Workhouse to Indian Military Hospital. Meanwhile, a third Indian hospital was coming more quickly into being in York Place where the schools there and in Pelham Street were being prepared to receive 550 patients. The result would be 'one of the cleanest, nicest, sweetest hospitals imaginable', complete with operating theatres, laundries and kitchens catering, like those at the Pavilion, for the various dietary requirements of different religious groups.

At last, on Saturday December 5th, the 'Gazette' could report the arrival at the Pavilion of the first small instalment of wounded Indians. They were put straight into the Music Room and the North Drawing Room. The first large contingent of 345 wounded arrived on Monday December 14th and, of these, 145 went to York Place and the rest to the Pavilion - 'Oriental patients', as the newspaper put it, for 'Dr Brighton'.

York Place clearly did its best to give its patients a friendly welcome though it naturally lacked the exotic appeal of the Pavilion. 'The Pavilion is more magnificent', the 'Gazette' admitted, 'but a very pleasant, home-like cheeriness has been established at York Place', and visitors remarked on the brightness of the former classrooms, now turned into wards, and the airy gym, now occupied by 60 beds.

Meanwhile, work was still going on at the old Workhouse. Janet Gooch, in her history of the Brighton General Hospital, has described how the Poor Law Institution was taken over in January 1915 and renamed the Kitchener Indian Hospital. When the military authorities carried out their inspection, they refused to accept the 177 bedsteads in the old infirmary as these were made of sacking and full of bugs. The one steam sterilizer was obsolete and the operating theatre was not a very modern one. With fresh equipment the hospital was first to be prepared to receive 1,500 patients, but by July the number of beds was increased to 2,000. Six wooden huts were pallisaded off in the grounds to form an isolation unit for 30 infectious cases. B Block provided 20 beds for what were known as 'insane cases' - that is, men suffering from shell-shock - and there were four padded cells. 60 Indian officers were to be nursed in a separate block.

For all the efforts expended 'the house on the hill' could never aspire to the obvious appeal of the Pavilion and the editor of the 'Gazette' was uncomfortably aware of it. Under the heading 'The Two Palaces' came the comment: 'There can be no getting away from the jarring note in the contrast. Never, perhaps, was there such a meeting of extremes'. Some consolation was sought in this unpromising situation: 'From the airy wards at the mansion on the ridge of the Downs the Indians will be able to look down on the domes and minarets of the Pavilion where their comrades are reposing as if in some soft, sequestered valley. The warriors at the Poor Law Institution will also enjoy the same bird's-eye view of the surrounding scenes on land and sea as the British wounded in the charming wards of the Grammar School on the other side of the valley, and perhaps they might arrange to exchange signals. It is a long way up Elm Grove; but it is to be hoped that the distance will not prevent hundreds of admirers from visiting this institution and cheering the Sons of the East'. These hopes would be put to the test when the first patients arrived at the Kitchener Hospital at the beginning of February.

Indian wounded in the grounds of the Royal Pavilion

Some men of the 15th Sikhs singing chants in a barn in Flanders. August. 1915 (Q 28,793)

The Indian Army in France

Following the offer of the Viceroy in 1914 to commit the Indian Army to the war, two infantry divisions, the 3rd (Lahore) and the 7th (Meerut), and one cavalry brigade, the 4th (Secunderabad), were mobilized on August 8th and ready to leave India two weeks later. After arriving in Egypt they heard that they were to be re-routed to Marseilles. The Expeditionary Force began disembarking on September 26th, still in the light khaki-drill uniforms suitable for service in Egypt. The troops had been accompanied from India by three clearing hospitals. Two of these - the Lahore and the Secunderabad - were established in France as General Hospitals and the third - the Meerut - was sent on to Brockenhurst in the New Forest.

Most of the units of the Indian Expeditionary Force would have arrived in France before October 10th when their Commander-in-Chief, Lieutenant-General Sir James Willcocks, issued his first Order of the Day. It was couched in the typically stirring terms thought appropriate at the time, to appeal to the men's sense of identity (religion, caste, region, regiment), to their task as warriors and to their personal loyalty to the King-Emperor:

'Soldiers of the Indian Army Corps
We have all read with pride the gracious message of His Majesty the King-Emperor to his troops from India . . . It is our firm resolve to prove ourselves worthy of the honour which has been conferred on us . . . You are the descendants of men who have been mighty rulers and great warriors for many centuries. You will never forget this. You will recall the glories of your race. Hindu and Mahomedan will be fighting side by side with British soldiers and our gallant French Allies. You will be helping to make history. You will be the first Indian soldiers of the King-Emperor who will have the honour of showing in Europe that the sons of

10

India have lost none of their ancient martial instincts . . . In battle you will remember that your religions enjoin on you that to give your life doing your duty is your highest reward. The eyes of your co-religionists and your fellow countrymen are on you. . . You will fight for your King-Emperor and your faith, so that history will record the doings of India's sons and your children will proudly tell of the deeds of their fathers'.

The soldiers would not have long to wait before showing their ancient martial instincts on the battlefield as they were soon involved in some of the earliest battles of the war.

The retreat from Mons and the fighting on the Marne and the Aisne and at Ypres during September and October were not so much battles as struggles for survival. By the end of 1914 the Regular soldiers of the BEF had suffered enormous casualties and those who were left, with the Territorials and a few Reservists, had the task of holding the line through the winter. It was, therefore, an understandable (if harshly brutal) decision to throw the Indian reinforcements straight into the field, ill-equipped and unacclimatised as they were. Within weeks they were at the Front, taking part in the bloody encounters in Flanders during November and December. The 129th Baluchis were the first to see action near Ypres on October 30th and Indian troops were heavily engaged before the end of the year around Givenchy and La Bassee. There they joined the attack on the Germans and suffered the furious counter-attack that followed.

Some Indian soldiers no doubt heard about the cease-fire which took place along parts of the front line over Christmas 1914. Many commentators have suggested that the British Tommy thought of 'old Jerry' in the trenches across No Man's Land as an ordinary man much like himself, 'to be bashed about when we had the chance', but with no real hatred, 'not even when we were heavily shelled'. The very idea of exchanging drinks and souvenirs, sharing food and playing football with the enemy would almost certainly have been incomprehensible to the Indian soldiers who were there to do their duty, and that meant to kill as many as possible of the enemies of the King-Emperor. The Germans certainly learnt a healthy respect for the fighting qualities of the Indian troops, and especially for the Gurkhas who seemed to have limitless courage and absolutely no fear.

By February 1915 the British casualties to date numbered well over 100,000. Back in Brighton the 'Gazette' published twice weekly its lengthening columns of names, under the heading 'The Price of War'. Increasingly the lists included those of the Indian dead, wounded or missing. In France the Indian Army fought on, around Neuve-Chapelle in March and at the 2nd Battle of Ypres from April 22nd to May 24th, when the Germans used poison gas for the first time. Also in May they were at Festubert and in June in the Argonne. In September the great Allied offensive took off in Champagne and the casualty lists following the Battle of Loos grew longer still. One of the missing in that battle was Rudyard Kipling's son, John. Such grievous losses among the Indian troops could not be sustained indefinitely. The hastily trained young recruits to Kitchener's army, as well as troops from the Dominions, were beginning to reach the battlefields in Europe and also the Near East, where the Gallipoli campaign claimed its thousands of victims. But the reinforcements on the Western Front could not make up the huge gaps in the Indian battalions and towards the end of the year the decision was taken to withdraw the greater part of the Indian forces from Europe for service on other fronts.

It is not surprising that morale among the Indians fell as the months passed. They had fought hard for over a year and sustained heavy losses. The replacements which arrived were conglomerations of drafts, and the strong identity of individual units, often originally made up very largely of kinship groups, was gone. As long as such groups from a single community were able to stay together they remained cheerful. One Lancer in the trenches wrote home: 'All of us from one village at home are assembled together and are very pleased with ourselves and always joking'. They fought alongside French and British soldiers who admired them but did not share their language or their ways. There was no home leave for the Indians at that time, and men became anxious when bad news came from India of sickness in their families or crop failures in their villages. Somehow their fighting spirit was maintained throughout, though - as in all armies - there were cases of self-inflicted wounds (the authorities soon became suspicious of the number of wounded left hands). There were even a few desertions. In March 1915 Jemadar Mir Mast and 14 Afridi Pathans deserted to the Germans and were made much of by enemy propaganda. But the men of the Indian Army were volunteers, highly selected and well trained - though for skirmishes on the North-West Frontier rather than battles on the fields of Flanders - and some positively enjoyed fierce fighting and did not fear death in battle. One man is quoted as saying, 'We took pleasure in the battle'. There were some for whom military service was a matter of honour, and the source of prestige not only for themselves but for their family, their caste or for their military family, the regiment. 'To die on the battlefield is glory. For a thousand years one's name will be remembered', wrote one in a letter home, and another wrote, 'Fighting is the work of brave men . . . Although their bodies are dead, their name and fame live for ever. Be, therefore, unconcerned'.

It was, above all, death with honour that would bring *izzat*, the reputation for honour that was so highly prized. Much has been written of the special relationship established between the Indian soldiers and their British officers. These officers, who knew the languages and ways of their men, generally did care deeply about their welfare, and there is plenty of evidence of mutual respect and loyalty. Nevertheless, it has been suggested that it was *izzat* which made men fight and lay down their lives in a cause they could not have understood. On the other hand, personal loyalty to the King-Emperor was something they did understand. George V was Colonel-in-Chief of ten Indian regiments and had said in 1906 that this was especially gratifying to him. At the great Indian Durbars of 1877, 1903 and most recently in 1911, the troops, Indian as well as British, played a very important part. For Indian soldiers in France or in the Military Hospitals in England a message or visit from the King was a great event. Even on December 1st 1914, as the King carried out an inspection in appalling weather, Indian troops gladly lined the road between Hinges and Locon.

The supreme honour was to receive an award from the King's own hands for feats of valour performed on the battlefield. There were hundreds of citations for honours, and five Victoria Crosses were awarded to Indian soldiers for their action in France. Six more were to be gained in other theatres of war. The first of these was awarded to Sepoy Khuda Dad Khan, and the second to Naik Darwan Sing Negi. The third was awarded posthumously to Rifleman Gobar Sing Negi, who was a member of the Garhwali Brigade leading an assault on the German trenches. He reached the fourth line of trenches and took command of his platoon when the commander was killed. The fourth, Jemadar Mir Dast, who was to be given his medal by the King at the Pavilion in Brighton, had rallied his men, held the position and helped to bring in eight wounded British and Indian officers, though himself wounded. (Ironically, it was his brother, Jemadar Mir Mast, who was one of the deserters mentioned above.) One more VC was gained by an Indian soldier at the Battle of Loos. The citation published in the 'London Gazette' on November 18th 1915 read as follows:

'VC Rifleman Kulbir Thapa - 3rd Gurkha Rifles - France 25/26 September 1915
For most conspicuous bravery during operations against the German trenches . . . when himself wounded, on the 25th September 1915, he found a badly wounded soldier of the Leicestershire Regiment behind the first line German trench, and, though urged by the British soldier to save himself, he remained with him all day and night. In the early morning of the 26th September, in misty weather, he brought him out through the German wire, and, leaving him in a place of comparative safety, returned and brought in two wounded Gurkhas, one after the other. He then went back in broad daylight for the British soldier and brought him in also, carrying him most of the way and being at most points under enemy's fire'.

12

The Gurkhas going into battle near near Neuve-Chapelle

It was not only the warriors who showed great courage. One account tells of a stretcher-bearer helping to carry in a wounded man. He had been badly hit by shrapnel but was just able to say: 'Put him down gently' before collapsing himself.

To behave with such conspicuous bravery in the heat of the battle takes a special kind of courage. Another kind of courage was required to endure constant danger, lack of sleep and freezing conditions in the water-logged trenches. One officer who agonized over his men was Captain Roly Grimshaw of the Poona Horse. Landing at Marseilles with his cavalry regiment on October 14th 1914, he described the early months of the war in his diary until he was himself wounded on December 20th and evacuated to England. Within twelve hours of arriving at the Front, he was shocked to see an ambulance 'filled with our fellows' after they had been sent out to dig support trenches. These were, incidentally, cavalry men who were not normally engaged in digging. The Colonel had been killed and about 45 men killed or wounded and a great many were missing since, owing to the darkness, many men got left behind. This was the situation that Grimshaw and his men found after de-training and marching to the front line. No wonder they were 'very shaken' with the casualties - about 20% of their fellows lost in one action.

The fact that so many men were missing, left behind in the darkness, is a reminder that the nights were filled with feverish activity. The wounded had to be evacuated and reinforcements of men and supplies brought up. Trenches had to be dug or shorn up, sandbags repaired or replaced, latrines cleared and barbed wire and communication wires laid or mended. There was continuous noise, not only from shells bursting or gunfire, but also the constant sound of picks and spades, digging machines and drainage pumps. The lunar landscape of No Man's Land was occasionally lit up by flares revealing stretcher-bearers trying to bring in wounded men or the bodies lying in the space between the two front lines.

The heavy rains of autumn 1914 were followed by severe frost and snow. The narrow trenches were often thigh-deep in freezing water or sticky mud. One Gurkha officer reckoned that the mud was their greatest enemy since it clogged the rifles and caused bayonets to fall off. It was impossible, he said, to climb up the wet sides of the trenches in many places and the men were often caught like rats in a trap. Roly Grimshaw actually rescued one of his own men who had slipped and disappeared. The 8th Gurkhas lost two men, drowned in their own trenches.

Amongst the hazards which the Indians faced were the unfamiliar European diseases, like measles, mumps and influenza. Added to these was the risk of contracting bronchitis and pneumonia as a result of being exposed to the damp cold of the trenches. Unclean drinking water caused enteric fever and dysentery. One of the worst problems was with the men's feet. Before the end of November snow had begun to fall, and the horses were issued with frost shoes. Grimshaw's men, however, had no extra protection for their feet and complained of the bitter cold. 'Some', Grimshaw recorded in his diary, 'simply flopped down in the mud . . . poor fellows!' Some asked to be left in the rain and mud, as their feet were too hopelessly bad to move. Grimshaw went off to arrange for them to be taken to hospital and was grateful to a French lorry driver who picked them all up. Frostbite, he believed, was infinitely more deadly than 'bullet bite', especially if gangrene set in. Grimshaw, in fact, saw some Gurkhas barefooted in the cold and asked them why they walked in bare feet. They replied, 'Sahib, our feet hurt us terribly, but in boots they hurt worse'.

At times when a unit was in the front line it was more important than ever that the men were properly fed. British officers in India were accustomed to respecting the religious and ritual requirements of their troops and extraordinary efforts were made in France to continue this practice. General Willcocks, writing after the war, described the arrangements:

'The rations consisted of meat for those who ate it, several days in the week . . . For non-meat eaters extra gur (sugar), dall (lentils), ghee (clarified butter), potatoes, tea, atta (flour) and five kinds of tasty ingredients: in addition, dried fruits such as raisins, etc. and various kinds of vegetables as procurable . . . Mixed sweetmeats were frequently supplied by friends and retired British officers . . . Rum was issued to those who were not prohibited from taking alcohol, and extra tea to those who could not indulge in the former. Goats were purchased from Southern Europe in large numbers; slaughtered at fixed stations on the line of communications by men of the various units; labelled with distinctive tapes and conveyed to destination by men of the different denominations. Nothing could have been more considerate than the details carried out to observe the customs of the sepoy; and Indian officers and men have said to me over and over again "The British Government is wonderful; here in the midst of the Mahabharat (great war) they even label our meat. Truly the Badshah (King) is a Rustam and a Hakim (a hero and a just man)" '.

Sometimes things did not go quite according to plan and John Masters, in 'Bugles and a Tiger', relates an incident in Flanders in 1914 when men of the 1st Battalion of 4th Gurkhas had had no food for a couple of days. When supplies at last reached the trenches they were found to consist of several hundred cans of corned beef, clearly marked with the company's trademark, a bull's head. No Hindu may eat beef, but there was nothing else on offer. The Colonel sent for the senior Gurkha officer, and wordlessly pointed to the rations. After a moment came the quiet reply, 'Sahib, we are here to fight the Germans. We cannot fight if we starve. It will be forgiven us. Remove the labels and let it be corned mutton'.

14

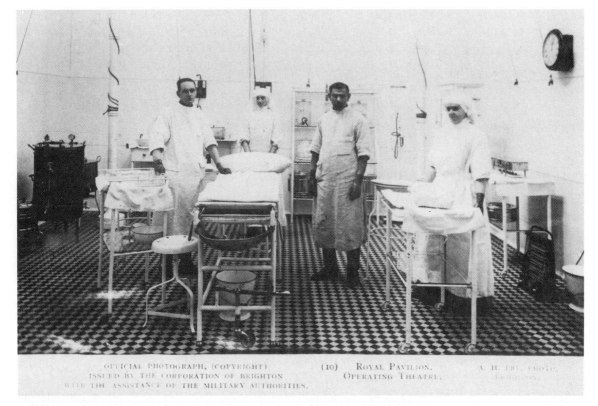

The Treatment of the Wounded

On Sunday December 20th 1914 Captain Grimshaw sat in the mud near Gorre, where the hospital had just received orders to evacuate, and waited with his men for the rations to come up. As they sat they watched the streams of wounded pouring past. 'The state of the wounded', wrote Grimshaw in his diary, 'beggars all description. Little Gurkhas slopping through the freezing mud . . . Tommies with no caps and plastered in blood and mud from head to foot; Sikhs with their hair all down . . . Pathans more dirty and untidy than usual; all limping or reeling along like drunken men, some helping an almost foundered comrade. In most cases misery depicted on their faces. Stretchers with groaning wounded and limping stretcher-bearers . . .'

There was, in fact, an elaborate system for evacuating the wounded from the Front. Each soldier carried with him, sewn to his uniform, a sterile first field dressing and this could be applied by the man himself or by someone nearby. If he was injured in No Man's Land he would probably have to wait until nightfall before being brought in. Rescue under fire was difficult and dangerous and demanded almost superhuman courage from the stretcher-bearers. The first to see the casualties were the Regimental Medical Officers who attended them in the trenches. The wounded men then walked, or were carried, to the Regimental Aid Posts at the rear. There the Medical Officer sorted the casualties. Field ambulances (mostly horsed) would take the wounded to the Advanced Dressing Stations for dressings to be adjusted and an anti-tetanus injection given. Motor ambulances would then convey them to another Dressing Station two or three miles to the rear.

By 1915 a light trolley line had been laid down to within little over a mile from the trenches. It brought up supplies and took away casualties. Patients would go on by train to one of the Clearing Hospitals some eight to ten miles behind the line, considered at a safe distance from

the fighting. These were often in breweries, convents or colleges taken over for the purpose. From there patients would go on by train for treatment in a Stationary or Base Hospital near to the coast before being returned to the trenches. More serious cases would be placed in a special Hospital Train to join the Hospital Ship to cross the Channel *en route* for a Military Hospital in England.

The original intention had been to nurse the Indian wounded in special hospitals in France. These were established at Merville and St Venant and there were places for 2,000 beds for Indian sick and wounded near Boulogne and Abbeville. These replaced an earlier arrangement to send them to a hospital in Marseilles. General Willcocks thought this had been a great mistake and commented on the folly of taking the wounded to a place where they would be seen by fresh drafts who would not be cheered on first arrival by meeting a lot of bandaged men. Within weeks of the start of the war the huge number of casualties made it impossible to find sufficient accommodation in France for the wounded Indians. General Willcocks was very much against their being brought to England, but since this was inevitable, plans were hastily made to provide hospital places for the Indians in the New Forest and at Brighton.

The Indian wounded, therefore, joined one of the six hospital trains that could each carry 400 patients at a time. The trains ran up and down behind the Front and along the coast to the ports where the Hospital Ships were waiting. The luckier patients were unloaded at Boulogne; the less fortunate faced a journey on to Le Havre, which was 200 miles away. At worst, this

16

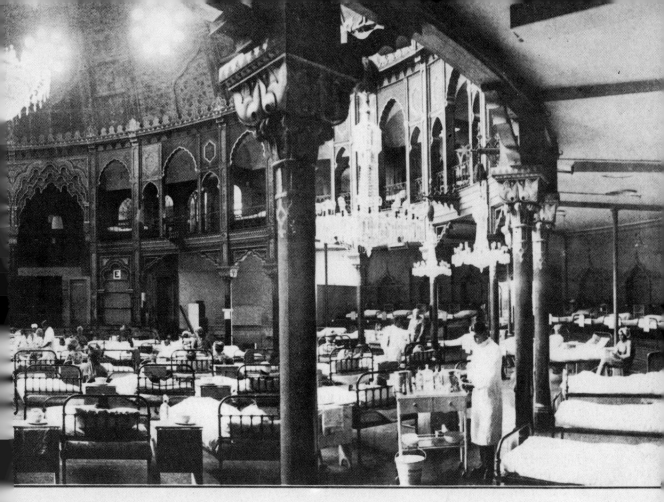

...om below the Balcony, on the North.

could take up to three days. Each train was specially equipped for cot cases as well as sitting patients and was staffed with two or three Medical Officers, four Nursing Sisters and 40 Orderlies, generally from the RAMC. Treatments, including surgery, could be continued on the train.

In one of her books Lyn Macdonald quotes from the diary of Sister Luard, who was attached to Hospital Train No 5. On November 25th 1914 she helped to care for a number of Sikhs, most of them wounded in the hand or arms. She was clearly moved with compassion for these men, so far from their homes and families, and admired 'their long, fine, dark hair under their turbans, done up with yellow combs; glorious teeth and melting, dark eyes'. She gave some of them morphia to relieve their pain and tried to comfort them with a few words of Hindustani 'picked up at a desperate pace'. It touched her that they should salaam after she had dressed their wounds on the long train ride to Le Havre. At this date the Sikhs must have been on their way to a hospital ship moored in Southampton Water or have gone to one of the hospitals already prepared for them in Brockenhurst. The Indian hospitals in Brighton were not yet ready to receive patients.

The first newspaper report of the arrival of a hospital train bringing Indian patients to Brighton appeared in the 'Gazette' of December 5th, though a few days earlier some Indian orderlies had moved into the Pavilion, creating much interest and comment from the local population. The first small contingent of wounded were placed straight away in the Music Room and the North Drawing Room. The authorities disapproved strongly of 'the crowds of women who cluster round every opening into the grounds' and responded by boarding up the openings. They also erected wooden screens around the railings. This did not stop some of the more curious from climbing up and perching on top of the fence - 'certainly not an edifying spectacle '.

By the time two full trainloads of 'Oriental Patients for Dr Brighton' arrived on Monday December 14th the whole town seemed ready to receive them. The trains were met by the Chief Constable and there were representatives of the RAMC, the Sussex VAD, the Red Cross and St John Ambulance to handle the 112 patients from the first train (100 of them stretcher cases) and 233 in the second, which had only a few stretcher cases. Crowds had gathered in the rain, where they stood and cheered these men all straight from the Front. Some ladies had arrived with 5,000 cigarettes. Long before there was any idea of the Indian wounded being brought to Brighton, the local newspapers had carried news of the Indians in France and there was general interest in them and affectionate gratitude to these 'Sons of the East' who had come to Britain's aid. Now the people of Brighton could show their appreciation.

The 'Gazette' editorial of December 16th expressed the feelings of the townspeople echoed in the words of the reporter - 'scenes of such amazing variety, of colour and animation . . . They find themselves in magnificent hospitals, with the pleasant ease of spring beds after the hardship of the trenches'. Part of the editorial reads as follows:

'At last the wounded Indians are duly installed at Brighton. They arrived under rather mournful conditions. A drab day, rainstorms, and a fierce sea running in the Channel, mud-laden streets, and a vista of dripping umbrellas and mackintoshes. That was the first impression the warriors got of Brighton, and it was rather chilling. But crowds assembled to voice public welcome, and the reception undoubtedly cheered the brave fellows. The hundred stretcher cases in the first train that reached the terminus on Monday afternoon constituted perhaps the most distressing of the many pathetic sights seen on similar occasions during the past four months. Something akin to a feeling of awe was created by the silence with which the work of bringing them out of the train and placing them in the motor ambulances was carried on'.

This moving scene was to be repeated many times in the months ahead and there always seemed to be a crowd to welcome and cheer the arrivals.

There was a special sense of pride in the fact that one of the first Indian VCs of the war, decorated by the King in France, was a patient at the Pavilion. The Havaldar, 'Gagna Singh', (the newspaper had some problems over the spelling of Indian names) of the 30th Garhwal Rifles had been injured in five places. 'One would have liked to be able to tell him in his own language', said the 'Gazette', 'that thousands of subjects of the King would be proud to shake hands with him'. Such a patient, to whom honour was due, was likely to find himself in that magnificent model Indian Hospital, the Pavilion, but normally new arrivals seem to have been placed in any one of the three hospitals where there were beds available. There is no evidence that there was any specialization in the treatment of injuries, except that the Kitchener had separate facilities for isolating the insane. All wards were mixed, with different religions and castes sharing the facilities though, as mentioned above, there were separate water taps for Hindus and Muslims and great care was taken to serve the appropriate food. There were special wards set aside for officers, and provision was made for religious worship in all three hospitals. The Corn Exchange was soon ready for occupation and some of the most serious cases were taken there. There was some movement of patients within the hospitals. 56 convalescents, originally quartered in the Pavilion, were shifted to cosily furnished ante-rooms off the Dome balcony. Some soon recovered their health and spirits. At York Place curious observers saw 'all sorts of the queerest romps going on with one patient carrying another on his back and others playing ball or leapfrog so far as bullet or shrapnel wounds would allow'.

19

INDIA'S FIGHTING MEN . PAVILION GROUNDS

The majority of cases were, in fact, gunshot wounds. The high-velocity bullet in use by 1914 could do much more damage than the low-velocity bullet of earlier wars. It could 'tumble' inside the body, splintering bone and damaging tissue. The multiple effects of bombs and especially shells were even more dangerous and often lethal. Shrapnel could cause several large or small rough wounds, the majority in the upper and lower extremities, and many resulting in fractures. The mental and physical effects of shell-shock resulted from the trauma of the explosion which could deafen or bury anyone close to it. One distressing case reported by the 'Gazette' was of a 'stalwart young Indian who had for the time become quite deranged as the result of his experience in the fighting lines'. After the 2nd Battle of Ypres, when the Germans used chlorine for the first time against men who were unprotected, there were many cases of gas poisoning. A further complication for men who had been wounded was that, as they fell to the ground, or were laid on straw before being removed to hospital, their wounds were infected by soil organisms from the heavily contaminated farmland. The available inoculations could not always prevent the development of tetanus or gas gangrene.

There was, therefore, very much that was new to the Medical Officers in the field or in the military hospitals as injuries were more severe and varied than in previous conflicts. There were good supplies of antiseptics, anaesthetics, dressings and instruments, and surgical techniques were highly developed. The practice of *debridement* (removal of damaged tissues) was well established by 1915, though blood transfusions were not common until 1917 (and anti-biotics did not come in until 1943). The value of warmth as a restorative was recognized by the establishment of *rechauffement* wards at the dressing stations. There were, of course, many amputations of limbs shattered by wounds, and feet or legs affected by gangrene - the result of trench foot. Amputations were generally carried out in France but sometimes it was necessary to perform a further operation after arrival in England.

There were, then, many kinds of different cases arriving at the hospitals in Brighton. Most of the patients were suffering from gunshot wounds and Janet Gooch tells us that nearly 2,000 of the cases admitted to the Kitchener Hospital were of this kind. All of these needed to be X-rayed on arrival and the X-ray equipment at the Kitchener was, it seems, out of date (before the war English hospitals had relied on imports of German-made tubes and it was some time before American supplies became available). The X-ray department at the Kitchener was set up using field service equipment and this included a wooden couch which was too short and not properly earthed, so that patients and operators often experienced electric shocks. At the Pavilion an X-ray room was attached to the operating theatre in the Dome.

In theatre wounds could be explored under anaesthetic and then drained. For this purpose quantities of dressings were required. These could be a very expensive item and, according to Janet Gooch, it became the practice to substitute sawdust pads or, very much more preferable, dressings made of dried sphagnum moss, supplies of which were obtained direct from Scotland and made into muslin-covered pads by ladies connected with the Indian Gift House. These pads were soft, compressible, partly deodorant and highly absorbent.

Near the main entrance to the Pavilion patients could receive treatment in small portable radiant heat baths or from instruments for giving local applications of electricity. As long ago as 1757 John Wesley recorded in his diary the use of an apparatus with which he 'ordered several persons to be electrified' and noted the remarkable cures from various disorders 'by virtue of this surprising medicine'. In 1852 a Brighton druggist, Thomas Mussell, was advertising 'Medical Galvanism', used 'to stimulate those nerves and muscles which a complete or partial paralysis has rendered dormant'. At the Pavilion Hospital patients could be given treatments involving galvanization, ionization or Faradization.

Medical and surgical treatment was given by British doctors and surgeons, most of whom were from the Indian Medical Service or the Civil Medical Service in India, and these would have had a knowledge of Hindustani and experience of working with Indians. The sub-assistant surgeons were Anglo-Indians and ward orderlies were drawn from either the RAMC or the IMS. 'Untouchables' were employed - and separately housed - to carry out the duties of sweepers and dhobis. The writers and clerks were Indians. All were under the supervision of Colonel R N Campbell who was in charge of the three Military Hospitals in Brighton.

The question of nurses arose when, in the early days, the Queen Alexandra's Imperial Military Nursing Service was expecting to provide staff for the Indian hospitals. The British in India were extremely sensitive about the status of white women, and the Viceroy, Lord Hardinge, made it clear that it was the usual practice not to employ any women in hospitals for Indian soldiers. This was also the view of General Willcocks. At the Pavilion and York Place, however, there were some European nurses in the early days but it was made clear that they were employed in supervisory duties only and did not do any of the actual nursing. At the Kitchener Hospital, opened in February 1915, no women were ever employed at all. Finally, in June 1915, the Army Council ordered that all the QAIMNS Reserve should be withdrawn from the Pavilion and York Place. No reason was given. Henceforth all the nursing was carried out by male orderlies. There was one interesting exception to this at Brockenhurst. The Lady Hardinge Hospital was not under the control of the War Office, and the 20 nurses employed there were not members of the nursing service but civilians under contract with some knowledge of an Indian language. Though requested by the War Office to withdraw these nurses, as had been done in other hospitals, the authorities in charge of the Lady Hardinge Hospital refused to conform and the nurses stayed. There was no scandal.

There were, of course, occasional deaths among the Indian patients, but these were few as severely wounded men often did not survive the long and agonising journey to England. Hindus and Sikhs who died at Brighton were cremated at a specially chosen site on the Downs near Patcham. Muslims were taken for burial in the grounds of the mosque which had been established at Woking since 1899.

6556 THE CHATTRI. PATCHAM. NR BRIGHTON. - JUDGES' LD.

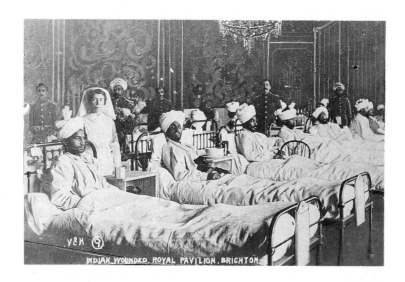

INDIAN WOUNDED, ROYAL PAVILION, BRIGHTON

Life in Hospital and Impressions of England

In the spring of 1995 a new play went into production at the Theatre Royal, Stratford East. 'Dusky Warriors', by Kulvinder Ghir and Nasser Memarzia, took as its theme the experience of the wounded Indians at Brighton during the First World War. Inevitably it was set in the exotic surroundings of the Pavilion (and, at the end of the Stratford run, given one poignant performance there in the Music Room) but a central part of the plot was based on an actual incident which took place, not there, but at the Kitchener Hospital. Janet Gooch records in her account of the Indian hospital in 1915 the attempted shooting by one of the sub-assistant surgeons of Colonel Sir Bruce Seton, who was in charge of the Kitchener. The case led to a court-martial and the man was sentenced to seven years' imprisonment.

It is clear that things were not as they should have been at the Kitchener Hospital, and although the official report recorded that discipline among the ward orderlies was good, there were problems among the followers, referred to as 'the sweepings of Bombay city'. Also mentioned were cases of drunkenness and the 'ill-advised conduct of women of the town'. Various kinds of restrictions on all personnel were introduced, barbed wire palings were fixed to the walls and the place was put under a military guard. Only the convalescent officers and the sub-assistant surgeons were free to go outside on their own; the other patients and hospital staff were sent out daily on a route march. Nothing like this appears to have happened at the Pavilion or York Place.

Two items reported in the 'Gazette' during July 1915 throw some light on problems at the Kitchener. The first was the case, later referred to the Assizes, of an alleged assault on a girl of 15 by one of the sub-assistant surgeons. The second report was headed 'Drink and Discipline. Kitchener's Hospital Affair'. The defendant, William Ford, was summoned for 'supplying whisky to Sandhu, an Indian member of HM Forces'. Sandhu had been on sentry duty and had given Ford two shillings and fourpence with which to purchase a bottle of whisky. Unfortunately for Sandhu, Colonel Campbell appeared at the wrong moment and took the bottle away. In giving evidence, Colonel Seton said that the several hundred Indian orderlies and attendants were not allowed to go into Brighton. He admitted 'It was probable that the men felt this restriction very keenly'.

Whatever the facts behind these events, the events certainly took place and suggest that the regime at the Kitchener under Colonel Seton was very different from that at the other Indian hospitals.

The message on the back of this card reads: 'From Miss Milman but not our visitors. This time another Lady's in the Crescent'. A Miss Milman lived at 13 Montpelier Crescent at this time.

There are in fact plenty of accounts of outings and picnics organised for the Indian patients, motor car rides and visits in Brighton to the Theatre de Luxe when a programme of films was being shown. On at least one occasion a party of convalescents from Brighton was taken on a day trip to London - news which caused Sir Walter Lawrence to voice his strong objections. But Sir Walter, in many ways the champion of the Indians in France, had always been against their coming to England at all, where he thought they were being somewhat spoilt and getting soft. Simply because 'the same care shown to the British wounded is extended to the Indians', there were liable to be misunderstandings, so that 'the fewer Indians who come to England the better for the Indian Army now and in the future'.

All this had much to do with Sir Walter's fears that contacts between the Indian soldiers and over-kindly English people would undermine the prestige carefully built up by the British as rulers of the Raj. In India there were strict codes to regulate all contacts between rulers and ruled and no ordinary Indian would expect to be entertained in the home of a European family. Particular anxieties surrounded possible encounters between Indian men and European women. There is evidence that in France there were plenty of women who found the Indians attractive and occasionally marriages resulted from such relationships. The Brighton newspapers refer significantly to the women who showed an excessive interest in the Indians. Some, no doubt, were prostitutes, but it is likely that the writers of 'Dusky Warriors' did not need to stray far from the facts when they introduced a love story between one of the Indian soldiers and a Brighton girl.

From the trenches in France, and from the hospitals in England, the soldiers sent letters to their families, written either by themselves or for them by their more literate comrades. These letters were translated from the various Indian languages into English for examination at the Censor's office in Boulogne. It is, of course, normal for soldiers' letters to be censored and the Indians may or may not have been aware of this. It is still possible to read these letters and to gain some understanding of the views of the men themselves and their feelings about their experience of life in hospital and the impressions they took away with them of England. There are many expressions of appreciation for the kindness and consideration shown to

them, the excellent treatment they received and the comfort of their surroundings. One sub-assistant surgeon, a Mahratti, wrote after visiting one of the larger hospitals where he found the patients were 'all quite happy and, seeing the arrangements there, I think everyone of them must be thanking God for having a bullet in their body. I really envied them. There were phonographs and pianos playing everywhere, fruits supplied in large amounts, clothes, etc, hand-carts for patients, and every possible comfort. The patients have become fat and plump'.

The Chief Censor wrote regular reports to Army HQ about the letters, assessing as nearly as he could the morale of the soldiers. He usually reported that the general tone was wonderfully good, and that the treatment and comfort of the patients was mentioned over and over again in terms of the warmest admiration. By January 1915, though, he began to detect that there was more evidence of depression. There was never any hint, he said, of resentment or anti-British feeling, and grumbling was almost entirely absent, but many more men were now giving 'a melancholy impression of fatalistic resignation to a fate that is regarded as speedy and inevitable'. The Censor tried to account for this by echoing Sir Walter Lawrence about the softness engendered by the mild regime of the hospitals (the unhappy situation at the Kitchener was yet to develop). The main reason, however, and a point brought out forcibly in 'Dusky Warriors', was that the first enjoyment of comfortable surroundings was 'being replaced by something approaching dismay when the men realised that many of them will be required to face again the horrors and discomforts of the present campaign'.

The men of the Indian Army were being treated in the same way as those wounded in the British Army - when fit they would be sent back to fight again in the trenches. Philip Mason and David Omissi both argue in their books that the contract entered into when the men were recruited obliged them to fight, and if necessary to die, in battle. But once that duty was fulfilled, according to their code, a man who had been wounded honourably in battle should not be sent to fight again. Sir Walter Lawrence understood this and recommended to GHQ that the wounded Indians should not be sent back to the Front, adding 'but they continued to be sent'. This was surely one essential point of disagreement between Sir Walter and his superiors, so perhaps it was not surprising that when Haig took command Sir Walter had to go.

THE KING AND QUEEN'S VISIT TO THE WOUNDED INDIANS AT BRIGHTON

Some of these feelings of depression were perhaps set aside as the people of Brighton did their best to cheer the men as they were convalescing. Various kinds of entertainments were arranged for them. One wonders what the Indians made of one concert which offered recitations, humorous songs at the piano and more songs by an English quartet of singers. They perhaps enjoyed more what followed when a number of patriotic lantern views were shown. Probably more to their taste was a unique matinee given in the Palace Pier Theatre by the Indian Art and Dramatic Society. 'The atmosphere of the unchanging East was speedily imparted by the opening prayer chanted by Pandit Shyama Shankar . . . garbed in Eastern robes of red and gold and uttering musical invocations to the divine triad'. This was followed by a conjurer performing magic tricks and a concert of Indian music 'played on strange instruments in wonderful harmonies'.

For the men in hospital, though, two things above all helped to give them pleasure - comforts and visitors. The crowds who came to watch the hospital trains being unloaded at Brighton station were accustomed to seeing the patients arrive, accompanied by bundles of considerable size. On one occasion in March it was reported that 'one man could scarcely lift some of the bundles seen on the platform . . . Two large vans were required to take them to the hospitals and the Indians are so intent on sticking to their possessions that it isn't always easy to coax them into letting go of them for a while'. Some of the objects in these bundles were war trophies (a German helmet, perhaps, acquired in the field) but many of the contents were comforts, sent out to France by the Indian Soldiers' Fund. These had sometimes caused problems at the Front, for, as General Willcocks wrote afterwards: 'vests, balaclaver (sic) caps, warm coats, goatskin overcoats, extra flannel shirts, socks, drawers, woollen mufflers and gloves poured into their kitbags until a man could neither put on nor even stagger under the burden, but the cry was "Still they come!" Kind ladies in England and Regimental Committees continued to send gifts for the Indian soldiers and I was obliged at last to cry a halt and find storage room for all that could not be moved forward from the rest billets'. Many of these comforts found their way back to Brighton and more gifts still poured in.

Most appreciated of all were the Christmas gifts from the King or other members of the royal family - a photograph, perhaps, or a handkerchief. Even better were His Majesty's actual visits to the soldiers in hospital. There were several of such visits to Brighton but the one which everybody remembered above all was that of August 15th 1915, when the VC was given to

25

Subadar Mir Dast. Queen Mary and Lord Kitchener accompanied the King on this occasion and a short movie film of this event can still be seen. Many of the most distinguished men of the day found their way at other times to the hospitals - always, of course, to the Pavilion, but also to York Place and the Kitchener. Sometimes, too, the men's own officers came to see them. Captain Roly Grimshaw was one who, when he had recovered from his wounds, stayed in Brighton in order to make several visits.

Among all the impressions made on these peasant farmers from the Punjab and hillmen from Nepal and the North-West Frontier there were some sights that were to be remembered especially vividly, and no doubt described equally vividly to their families.

'Shortly before the closing of the hospitals some Indian soldiers were asked which of all the wonders they had seen in Brighton they considered the most remarkable. After some reflection they explained that the sight which had most aroused their wonder and admiration was the working model, in a glass case, exhibited by its creator, an elderly retired miner, which stands on the cliff near Black Rock. The model in question represents small figures of men at a pithead . . . On the clockwork being set in motion, the blacksmith nails in the horse's shoe, his assistant blows the bellows, men work their picks, and others severally perform their various occupations. It is curious that this model which would scarcely claim the attention of the ordinary passer-by should have been considered by these Indian soldiers to be the most wonderful sight in the "Queen of Watering Places" '.

Long after the men returned to India the memories and impressions remained. Subadar Mir Dast VC was in hospital in Bombay when he was interviewed by 'The Times of India'. His remarks under the headline 'Indian VC's Appreciation' show the more positive sides of the experience.

'I received the kindest of treatment. People of rank and the greatest soldiers and statesmen came and they talked so nicely to me. They expressed their admiration for the work done by the Indian soldiers in the field. Lastly, my happiness was crowned by the visit of his Majesty the King-Emperor. My heart was filled with joy and gratitude when his Gracious Majesty with his own hands pinned the Victoria Cross on me, shook hands with me and congratulated me on winning the distinguished order. The King spoke in English and his speech was translated to me by a British officer in Hindustani. The purport of it was that he was highly pleased with the valour of the Indian Army and it gave him the greatest pleasure to decorate brave Indian soldiers. Another visit gave me equal pleasure. It was from the Queen Mother, Queen Alexandra, who condescended to come and see me'.

'How did you like the treatment from your British comrades?' the Subadar was asked. 'Splendid. They treated us like brothers, even more than brothers. For it is a fact to which the whole Indian Army in the field can testify most gratefully that whenever soldiers fell wounded on the field the British soldiers first removed the Indian wounded soldiers to the hospital and then the British soldiers. They are really noble and chivalrous fellows. Our British officers, too, were very kind. They made no distinction between the British, the Mahometan or the Hindu soldiers - all were treated alike'.

1916 Farewell to the Indians

From time to time the 'Gazette' reported not the arrival but the departure of Indian soldiers. Some went for convalescence to a seaside resort near the New Forest. Others, too badly wounded to fight again, returned to their homes or hospitals in India. Those who were restored to health went, in spite of General Willcocks' plea, back to France or shortly afterwards to Mesopotamia. Some units of the Indian Cavalry remained in France throughout the war and their wounded were treated in hospitals there. The Indian Labour Corps was kept in Europe after the main body of the Indian contingent had left. It was engaged in navvying, road-building and mending, tree-felling and work on the railways, releasing fighting soldiers for service on the Front. Following the departure of the Indians from Brighton, the military hospitals were used by British and Dominion wounded.

The departure of the Indians was marked at the Pavilion by the decision in January 1916 to throw the whole place open to the public in aid of the Mayor of Brighton's War Charities. At last the Pavilion was to yield up its closely guarded mysteries and allow the townspeople 'to inspect the special arrangements necessitated by difference of caste and creed, and see how admirably in every respect the soldiers were cared for during the time they were patients of Dr. Brighton'. On the Monday of the first week of February visitors paid 2s 6d to go all over the buildings to see what they looked like when the Indians were in possession. On the Tuesday, Wednesday and Thursday (all one shilling days) there were 737, 709 and 695 paying visitors, and on the Friday, when the charge was reduced to sixpence, 2,675 people queued right through Castle Square to the Steine to get in, passing by the pay-box at a rate of 15 a minute. But even this record was broken on the Saturday when the queue stretched right round the grounds inside the gate as people stopped to take in the details of arrangements of various kitchens. By February 9th there had been over 10,000 visitors. Many of them bought at least one of the two official publications available, both written by Henry D Roberts. One, priced sixpence, was entitled 'The Story of the Royal Pavilion, Brighton, including a description of it as a Hospital for Indian Wounded Soldiers'. The other, with 120 pages and 35 illustrations, cost one shilling and included translations of the text into Urdu, Hindustani and Gurmukhi. The India Office purchased 20,000 copies of this publication for distribution in India. Picture postcards showing the wards and scenes in the grounds could be bought for twopence each.

The 'Gazette' for Wednesday February 2nd gave a full account of what the visitors could see and contrasted the orderly scene which would meet their eyes with the more animated appearance of the hospital in its early days.

'The wards are now all beautifully tidy - as they were not always when the Indians were there, at least in the first weeks of the historic hospital. Those who went through the Pavilion then will ever remember the picturesque confusion which everywhere met the eye. It was truly Eastern; and the Indians seemed to enjoy themselves vastly among all the heterogeneous litter of things inconceivable in Western domesticity. Sir Walter Lawrence, Bart, the Commissioner for Indian Hospitals, soon did wonders with the magic wand of order; and then came Colonel Neil Campbell CB, CIE as Senior Medical Officer, assisted by a most competent staff. The result was one of the most perfectly managed hospitals in the world. Untidiness was unknown; everything was spick and span; and the friendliest feeling always prevailed. An experiment of extreme difficulty was carried out with complete success'. It is to be hoped that the Indians themselves appreciated the tidying up of their cherished possessions.

The public was now urged to take advantage of this last chance to inspect the Pavilion as an Indian hospital.

'The magnificent State apartments, the smaller rooms, the Dome and the Corn Exchange are still to be seen as the gallant Eastern soldiers left them. The beds stand in white array, with the little table beside each, and all the facilities introduced for caste and ritual observances. Everything is brilliantly neat and clean. It is a pleasure to go through the wards, for the Indian atmosphere lingers, though the men have nearly all gone. A few Indians are still too ill to be moved, and the medical and nursing staffs have therefore not been quite disbanded. Several Indian orderlies and a number of British orderlies were about the place on Monday, and all of them were most courteous and helpful in directing visitors . . . The praying-tent, before the looped-up drapings of which the King and Queen and their entourage stood looking in at the wonderful scene of Eastern worship, has been removed, as there is no longer any need for it, the sacred accessories having been taken away by the Indians; but the site is boldly marked and there is hardly a piece of ground in the British Isles which appeals more strangely to the historic imagination'.

In November 1920 there was a sale by auction to dispose of furniture and equipment no longer needed once the hospitals had finally closed. One odd item reminded those present of the Indian soldiers who had come and gone. It was Lot 529: 'Mahomadon rolling pin, 6 lemon-squeezers, sauce tureen body and soup tureen cover'.

Indian wounded soldiers in the grounds of the Royal Pavilion

In Memoriam

In February 1917 the 'Gazette' made the first mention of the scheme for an Indian memorial on the Downs near Brighton, to mark the place where the Hindu and Sikh dead had been cremated. The memorial - now known as the Chattri - was not to be erected until after the war, when it was unveiled by the Prince of Wales. The inscription, in Urdu, Hindi and English reads: 'To the memory of all Indian soldiers who gave their lives for their King-Emperor in the Great War, this monument, erected on the site of the funeral pyre where the Hindus and Sikhs who died in hospital at Brighton passed through the fire, is in grateful admiration and brotherly affection dedicated'. Today the Chattri can be seen from many parts of the town - a white memorial within an area of green, marked off by a square of trees.

There are no graves of Indian soldiers at Brighton, though several may be found in the churchyard of St Nicholas at Brockenhurst. In a number of the cemeteries maintained by the War Graves Commission in northern France are the graves of many Indians who were killed, alongside those of the British dead, and near to Neuve-Chapelle - the scene of some of the bloodiest engagements in which the Indian Corps took part - there is an impressive memorial to the Indian dead. It attracts to the present day visitors of many nationalities who record in the Book of Remembrance their tributes to the men who died so far from home.

Some of the regiments which fought in France during the war gained battle honours to commemorate particular actions. The 9th Royal Deccan Horse fought at Givenchy in 1914, at the Somme in 1916 and at Bazentin, Delville Wood, Flers-Courcelettes and Cambrai in 1917. Some regiments commemorate annually a particular date in their history. The 4th Gurkhas chose as its Regimental Day March 11th, officially known as Neuve-Chapelle-Baghdad Day, but just called Neuve-Chapelle Day by the men of the 1st Battalion. The 2nd Punjab Regiment, in the front line at Loos, chose to commemorate Loos Day each year with a ceremonial parade.

29

Back in Brighton there was to be another reminder of the Indian soldiers. On October 26th 1921, Major-General H H the Maharajah of Patiala unveiled and dedicated the Indian Memorial Gateway at the south entrance to the Royal Pavilion. It had been erected 'by Subscriptions from certain Indian Princes and gentlemen as a permanent record of their gratitude for the care and attention shown to the Indian soldiers in the three Indian Military Hospitals in Brighton'. The inscription today only mentions the Pavilion. Hundreds of Brightonians and visitors to the town daily pass this gateway, some perhaps on their way to the Art Gallery in the Museum where they may see two paintings by CHH Burleigh, one of 'The Music Room as a Hospital for Indian Soldiers' and the other 'The Dome as an Indian Military Hospital'. (Another painting by Burleigh of the Banqueting Room may be seen at the Imperial War Museum, and a fourth is at the Tate Gallery, showing the operating theatre at the Dome.)

The most impressive commemoration in Brighton, however, was that which, until recently, took place at the Chattri annually on one Sunday afternoon in June. For 75 years since the Chattri was unveiled by the then Prince of Wales in 1921, a pilgrimage was made from Patcham up over the Downs to the memorial. This event, organised by the local branch of the British Legion, was attended by numbers of Brighton people, including dignitaries of the town and county, and many visiting Indians came to witness the wreath-laying and to hear the Last Post sounded. After the Reveille a reception was held at which representatives of the Indian High Commission were present. Though this elaborate ceremony will no longer be held, the Chattri still stands to remind residents and visitors alike of the Indian soldiers who fought in France in the early months of the First World War, and who, when wounded, stayed for a time in the three military hospitals in Brighton.

(3) G·A·WILES BRIGHTON
DEDICATION OF THE INDIAN CHATTRI BY H·R·H· THE PRINCE OF WALES ON THE DOWNS PATCHAM FEB 1 1921

'Our Indian wounded soldiers at Brighton'. Thought to be outside 1 - 3 Grand Parade

A Note on Sources

My interest in the Indian Expeditionary Corps arose from seeing the Chattri on the Downs and reading about the arrival and departure of the Indian wounded between December 1914 and January 1916 in the 'Brighton Gazette ' and other local newspapers. Their files are available in the Brighton Reference Library. Henry D Roberts gives more detailed information about the Pavilion in 'The Story of the Royal Pavilion, Brighton, Including a Description of it as a Hospital for Indian Wounded Soldiers' (1916). There is a useful chapter on the Kitchener Hospital in Janet Gooch's 'A History of Brighton General Hospital' (1980). 'The Indian Army' by Lieutenant-General S L Menendez (New Delhi 1993) is a general history which includes a discussion of theories about the martial races.

Philip Mason's 'A Matter of Honour' (1974) is a history of the Indian Army in which he includes excerpts from letters sent by Indian soldiers from France and England during the Great War. David Omissi's 'The Sepoy and the Raj' (1995) gives a critical account of the relationship between the Indian soldiers and their British officers and makes use of the soldiers' letters to examine the morale of the men in the trenches and hospitals from 1914 to 1916. Translations of the letters themselves and the reports of the Chief Censor are to be found in the British Library (Oriental and India Office Collections). These provide an invaluable source for any understanding of the Indians' feelings about their experience of the war.

Official accounts of their experience from the points of view of the British commanders may be found in 'The Indian Corps in France' (1919) by Lieutenant-Colonel J W B Merewether and Sir Frederick Smith. General Sir James Willcocks, whose name occurs often in this account, published 'With the Indians in France' in 1920. The views of one British officer with the Indian Cavalry may be found in the diary of Captain Roly Grimshaw, published under the title of 'Indian Cavalry Officer 1914-15" (1986). Grimshaw also includes a fictitious account which purports to have been written by one of the Indian soldiers who was treated at the Pavilion Hospital in Brighton.

John Turner provides a useful background in 'Britain and the First World War' (1988) and Barbara Tuchman's 'August 1914' (1962) and three books by Lyn Macdonald - 'The Roses of No Man's Land' (1985), '1914-1918: Voices and Images of the Great War' (1988) and '1915; The Death of Innocence' (1993) - all contribute to some understanding of the war during 1914 and 1915 and include allusions to the part played by the Indian Corps in France. I also learnt a great deal about the First World War from a series of lectures given at a summer school by Dr Gary Sheffield and I was especially grateful to him for suggesting and supplying me with further reading.

Among other books I have found useful are Kenneth Ballhatchet's 'Race, Sex and Class under the Raj' (1980), Brereton on 'The Great War and the RAMC' (1918), John Gaylor's 'Sons of John Company. The Indian and Pakistani Army 1903-1991' (1992), John Laffin's 'Surgeons in the Field' (1970) and Donald McDonald's 'Surgeons Two and a Barber, being some account of the Life and Work of the Indian Military Services, 1600-1947' (1950).

I am grateful to the staffs of Brighton Reference Library, the British Library (India Office Collections), the Gurkha Museum, the Imperial War Museum, the Lymington Public Library, the National Army Museum and the Wellcome Institute for the History of Medicine. All have given me help in finding books and tracing sources. Heather Lyster assisted me in finding information about the Indian wounded who were treated in and near the New Forest.

All errors, of fact or interpretation, are, of course, my own. JC

The Indian memorial at Neuve-Chapelle

Note on Ranks in the Indian Army
Havildar : Indian NCO (Sergeant)
Jemadar : Indian Company officer (Lieutenant)
Naik : Indian NCO (Corporal)
Risaldar : Indian cavalry officer
Sepoy : Indian infantry private
Sowar : Indian cavalry trooper
Subedar : Senior Indian officer in infantry company
Subedar major : Senior Indian officer in infantry battalion

The spelling of Indian words
Spellings of Indian words are quoted as given in the original sources and are therefore not necessarily consistent. Today's Muslim might be known as a Mohammedan, Mahomedan, Mohometan or Mahomadon.

Acknowledgements

This book was compiled by Selma Montford, Jacqueline Pollard and Robert Sanderson.

We are grateful to the following people and organisations for having allowed us to use photographs from their collections: Peter Booth; Brighton Museum; Janet Gooch; Tony McKendrick-Warden; Newhaven Historical Society (based at the Local and Maritime Museum at Newhaven); Jacqueline Pollard; Vanessa Sykes; and to Robert Sanderson for copying some of the photographs.

The photograph on page 10 is Crown Copyright of the Imperial War Museum.

Brian V Thomas generously permitted the use of the photographs on page 32 and on the back cover, taken in France of the Indian memorial at Neuve-Chapelle.

We are grateful for the support and encouragement we have received from the following members of staff at Brighton Museum: John Roles, Principal Keeper Collections and Local History; Jacqueline Frisby, Assistant Keeper Local History and Archaeology and Caroline Cook, Assistant Keeper of Non-Western Art and Anthropology.

© Joyce Collins

First published in 1997 by Brighton Books (Publishing)

c/o ETP, 9 South Road, Brighton BN1 6SB 'Phone & Fax: 01273-542660

email streetwise@pobox.com

ISBN 1-901454-01-0

Part of the proceeds from the sale of this book will be sent to the Gurkha Welfare Trust

Printed by Delta Press, 2 Goldstone Street, Hove, East Sussex BN3 3RJ

About Brighton Books (Publishing)
The Vanishing Villas of Preston & Withdean (1996) Brighton Books (Publishing) no 1
available from the address above @ £5.50 + £1 p & p

The following books are also available from Brighton Books:
'Back Street Brighton' (1989) about Brighton in the 1950s £3.95
'Brighton Behind the Front' (1990) about Brighton in the Second World War £3.95
'Blighty Brighton' (1991) about Brighton in the First World War £4.95
'D-Day : Brighton Remembers' (1994) £3.00
'Past & Present : the story of Blaker's Park' (1995) £3.00

Please add £1 per book, £3 for 3 books or more, for postage & packing

Cheques should be made payable to Brighton Books (Publishing) with the cheque card number on the back

End papers: Wounded Indians in the grounds of the Royal Pavilion with the Dome in the background

Back cover: the Indian memorial at Neuve-Chapelle

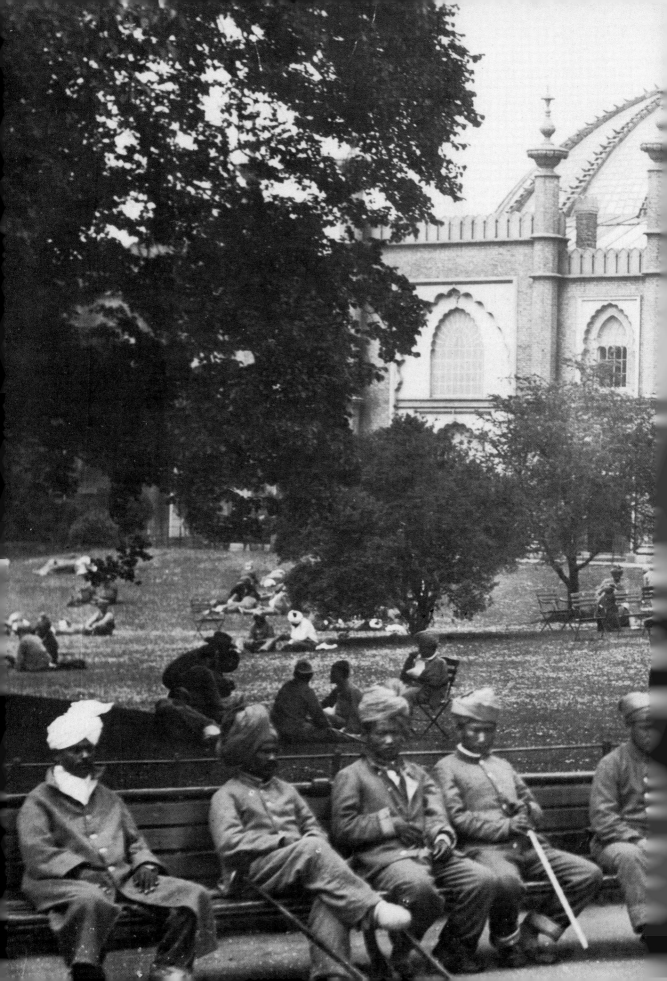